J
341.237

S0-AEQ-056

Wapiti regional library

CANADA AND THE UNITED NATIONS

BEV CLINE

JMCPL
DISCARDED

Weigl

Published by Weigl Educational Publishers Limited
6325 10 Street SE
Calgary, Alberta, Canada
T2H 2Z9

Website: www.weigl.com

Copyright ©2010 WEIGL EDUCATIONAL PUBLISHERS LIMITED
All rights reserved. No part of this publication may be reproduced, stored in a retrieval system, or
transmitted in any form or by any means, electronic, mechanical, photocopying, recording, or otherwise,
without the prior written permission of the publisher.

Library and Archives Canada Cataloguing in Publication data available upon request.
Fax 403-233-7769 for the attention of the Publishing Records department.

ISBN 978-1-55388-966-3 (hard cover)
ISBN 978-1-55388-969-4 (soft cover)

Printed in the United States of America
1 2 3 4 5 6 7 8 9 0 13 12 11 10 09

All of the Internet URLs given in the book were valid at the time of publication. However, due to the
dynamic nature of the Internet, some addresses may have changed, or sites may have ceased to exist
since publication. While the author and publisher regret any inconvenience this may cause readers, no
responsibility for any such changes can be accepted by either the author or the publisher.

Weigl acknowledges Getty Images as its primary image supplier for this title.
Printed with permission from the Department of National Defence and Library and Archives Canada:
page 12 left.

Every reasonable effort has been made to trace ownership and to obtain permission to reprint copyright
material. The publishers would be pleased to have any errors or omissions brought to their attention so
that they may be corrected in subsequent printings.

We acknowledge the financial support of the Government of Canada through the Book Publishing
Industry Development Program (BPIDP) for our publishing activities.

EDITOR: Heather C. Hudak
DESIGN: Terry Paulhus

Canada and the United Nations
Contents

Canada and the United Nations
Through The Years

I n 1967, during its centennial year, Canada hosted Expo 67. The event was also known as "Man and His World." One display that attracted a great deal of interest from Canadians was the United Nations Pavilion, with the flags of its members waving in the wind. Canadians were eager to find out how Canadian participation, leadership, and talent have helped the UN to make the world a safer, better place for all people.

The United Nations operates as a family of organizations. This is known as the United Nations "system." The Secretariat, headed by the Secretary-General, is the head of a vast organization of people that carry out the day-to-day operations of the United Nations from its headquarters in New York City.

These include administering peacekeeping operations, mediating international disputes, and preparing studies on human rights or the environment.

The UN members meet in what is called the General Assembly, which is like a world parliament. Each member, whether it is a developed or developing country, or if it has a large or small population, has only one vote. There is also the Security Council, a group of 15 members that is responsible for maintaining peace and security around the world. Canada has a Permanent Mission in New York that is staffed by diplomats who represent Canada's interests in the United Nations.

2000

Canada Ranked Number One

In 2000, Canada ranked right at the top of the United Nations Human Development Index for the seventh year in a row in terms of adult literacy. Canada scored a 99 percent rate. The ability to read is considered to be so important for personal success in life that, in 1965, the United Nations Educational, Scientific and Cultural Organization (UNESCO) established September 8 as International Literacy Day. Each year across Canada, schools and communities hold book fairs, library events, contests and reading festivals where authors of children's books read aloud and talk about their writing.

Canada Ranked Number One

Human Development Index

The United Nations Development Programme (UNDP) produces a report called the Human Development Index. It assesses countries based on the life expectancy of its citizens, availability of education, and standard of living. This chart shows the top 10 countries for 2006.

Country	Value
1. Iceland	0.968
2. Norway	0.968
3. Canada	0.967
4. Australia	0.965
5. Ireland	0.960
6. Netherlands	0.958
7. Sweden	0.958
8. Japan	0.956
9. Luxembourg	0.956
10. Switzerland	0.955

Canada Ranked Number One

2001

The United Nations and UN Secretary-General Kofi Annan are jointly awarded the Nobel Peace Prize.

2002

The International Year of Mountains is declared.

2000s

United Nations Millennium Declaration

In 2000, leaders from UN member states, including Canada, gathered at UN headquarters in New York City. Although many of them did not agree with every action the UN or its agencies took, they reaffirmed their faith in the UN's ability to play a central role in creating a more peaceful, prosperous, and just world. This meeting resulted in the United Nations Millennium **Declaration**. It set a number of ambitious goals for helping the world's poorest people. These included drastically reducing world poverty, hunger, and disease by 2015. The goals also included working to make sure that every boy and girl in the world can get a primary education.

United Nations Millennium Declaration

2003	2004	2005
The International Year of Freshwater is declared.	Louise Arbour is appointed UN High Commissioner for Human Rights.	Canada hosts a United Nations Climate Change Conference in Montreal.

PARTAGEZ LA ROUTE

SHARE THE ROAD

2008

International Year of Languages

"Languages matter!" is the slogan used by the United Nations Educational, Scientific and Cultural Organization (UNESCO) to highlight the importance of preserving languages. It is estimated that more than 50 percent of the 6,700 languages spoken around the world are threatened with extinction. Canada has a rich history of French, English, and Aboriginal languages. As well, many Canadian schoolchildren have parents or grandparents who came here from other countries. Languages let people communicate with each other and are important in keeping different cultures and traditions alive. Language has even been called the living heritage of humanity.

2006

CANIMUN 2006 is the world's largest bilingual Model UN.

2007

The UN International Labour Organization hosts an event called "Decent Work for Persons with Disabilities."

Canadian National Peacekeepers Day

2008

Canadian National Peacekeepers Day

Canada's international peacekeepers were honoured on the first-ever National Peacekeepers Day, held in Ottawa on August 9, 2008. On that date in 1974, nine Canadian peacekeepers died, the largest number to die on a single day. Canada has a proud tradition of peacekeeping. Former Canadian Prime Minister Lester B. Pearson is often called the "Grandfather of Peacekeeping." He devised the idea of using international peacekeeping forces from United Nations countries to try to contain or end conflicts in other nations around the world.

2009

Red Hand Day

On Red Hand Day, February 12, children in many schools across Canada made red handprints on paper and banners. The red hand is the symbol of the international effort to end the use of child soldiers. In many countries, even in some countries that have pledged to the United Nations that they will not allow children to be recruited as soldiers, children are still being forced into conflict against their will. In 2009, young people from 101 countries collected more than 250,000 red hands and presented them to UN Secretary-General Ban Ki-moon at UNICEF House in New York.

Red Hand Day

Into the Future

In 2001, the United Nations set September 21 as the International Day of Peace. The United Nations asks children around the world to send in their ideas as to how peace can be achieved, so that these ideas can be presented to world leaders. Many Canadian children and school classes have sent in their suggestions. How do you think you or your school could celebrate International Peace Day? How can you contribute to peace in your community and around the world?

2008
The UN celebrates the 60th anniversary of its Universal Declaration of Human Rights.

2009
The United Nations proclaims 2009 as the "International Year of Astronomy."

Canada and the United Nations
1990s

World Summit for Children

1992

Earth Summit

Leaders from government and organizations concerned about the effects of climate change met in Rio de Janeiro, Brazil. They talked about the effects of economic development on the world. They wanted to find ways to stop pollution and the destruction of natural resources. The name of the meeting was the United Nations Conference on Environment and Development, but it is usually referred to as the Earth Summit. Canada was a strong supporter of the summit. Canada's Maurice Strong was the Conference Secretary-General. Canada was also the first industrialized country to **ratify** the United Nations Convention on Biological Diversity, the first ever global agreement on biological diversity, which was created at the summit.

1990

World Summit for Children

The care and protection of the world's children has always been a priority for the United Nations. In 1989, the United Nations created 54 principles that make up the Convention on the Rights of the Child. These rights include the right to a name and nationality, to education, to play, and special rights for children who are disabled. A year later, the largest gathering of world leaders ever to come together up to that time met to continue their work to make the world a better place for children. They sat around an immense circular table at the United Nations headquarters in New York and talked about the world's responsibilities to children in both rich and poor countries.

Canada was one of six countries who had called for the summit, and the country co-chaired the event. The result of this summit was the World Declaration on the Survival, Protection and Development of Children. "We do this," the leaders declared, "not only for the present generation, but for all generations to come."

Earth Summit

1991
The General Assembly adopts the MI Principles for the protection of persons with mental illness.

1992
Leaders at the Earth Summit outline goals for sustainable development in the 21st century.

Secretariat of the Convention on Biological Diversity (SCBD)

1992

Reconciliation: The Peacekeeping Monument

In 1992, more than 2,000 Canadian peacekeepers paraded through the streets of Ottawa. They were attending a ceremony to unveil a new monument honouring their peacekeeping activities around the world. **Reconciliation**, the only monument of its kind in the world, honours the more than 110,000 Canadian peacekeepers who have served in zones of conflict around the world. The monument's three peacekeepers, two men and a woman, stand on two sharp, knifelike edges of stone, cutting through the rubble and debris of war and converging at a high point, which symbolizes the resolution of conflict.

1996

Secretariat of the Convention on Biological Diversity (SCBD)

Since 1996, Montreal has been the home of the Secretariat of the Convention on Biological Diversity (SCBD). The SCBD supports the goals of the convention. Many countries have donated artworks that represent their rich and unique cultural heritage and their relationship to biological diversity to the Museum of Nature and Culture. The museum is located in the Secretariat's offices.

Reconciliation: The Peacekeeping Monument

1993
Canada names November 20 as Child Day.

1994
Pearson Peacekeeping Centre opens in Nova Scotia to train international peacekeepers.

1995
The UN celebrates its 50th birthday.

11

Canadian Peacekeeping Service Medal

The Nobel Peace Prize was awarded to all United Nations peacekeepers in 1988. This inspired the creation of the Canadian Peacekeeping Service Medal to acknowledge the unique contribution to peace that Canadian peacekeepers have made since 1947. The medal shows an unarmed observer and two Canadian Forces soldiers, a man and a woman. The ribbon for the medal is comprised of four colours. These are green, red, white, and United Nations blue. Blue and white are the colours of the United Nations, the organization under which the majority of peacekeeping and observer missions have occurred. Red and white are for the Canadian flag. The green represents the idea of **volunteerism**.

Canadian Peacekeeping Service Medal

1998

Louise Fréchette

Imagine being appointed as the second in command of the United Nations. That is what happened to Canadian diplomat Louise Fréchette. In 1998, the United Nations decided to create the new position of United Nations Deputy Secretary-General. Fréchette was selected for this prestigious job, making her responsible for one of the most influential institutions in the world. Montreal-born Fréchette had worked hard and gained a great deal of international experience. She used this experience while representing Canada at the UN and as Canada's Deputy Minister of National Defence. In 1998, she was also appointed as an Officer of the Order of Canada.

1999

Ottawa Treaty

Every year, in many countries where there have been wars, anti-personnel landmines left in the ground kill or injure innocent people walking or playing outside. Across the world, many people demanded that something be done about the problem. By the mid-1990s, international negotiations to limit landmines through the UN Convention on Certain Conventional Weapons in

Louise Fréchette

1996
The UN Trust Fund in Support of Actions to Eliminate Violence Against Women is created.

1997
Canadian schoolchildren share their Peace Day plans with the UN.

1980 had ground to a halt. That is when Canada decided to step in and lead the world in the effort. In 1996, Canada announced an immediate **moratorium** on the use, production, trade, or export of anti-personnel mines. Canada also offered to host an international conference in Ottawa where plans could be made to completely ban anti-personnel mines. Canada then issued a challenge to the world to negotiate and sign a treaty to ban landmines in 14 months, a process that can often take years. Faced with this challenge, the world responded positively. By 1999, 40 countries had agreed to the Ottawa Treaty, making it international law. It had been ratified faster than any other treaty in history. Today, though landmines are still in use, many countries are aware of the threat they pose to civilian life, and efforts continue to make mined areas safe again.

Ottawa Treaty

Into the Future

If you have ever asked "What can I do?" to help improve the world, former UN Secretary-General Kofi Annan has an answer. "When you see something wrong, no matter how big the problem is, think: Who else would like to change this? How can we work together?" If you could focus on one or two ways to improve the lives of children around the world, even in a small way, what would these be? What actions would you take?

1998
The Universal Declaration of Human Rights has its 50th anniversary.

1999
The first World Space Week takes place in October.

2000
The UN declares the International Year for a Culture of Peace.

Canada and the United Nations
1980s

Canada's National Anthem

1980

Canada's National Anthem

Although Canadians had been singing "O Canada" at schools and public events in Canada and around the world for decades, it was only proclaimed Canada's national anthem on July 1, 1980. Thousands of Canadians gathered on Parliament Hill to hear Governor General Edward Schreyer proclaim the act that made the song an official symbol of Canada. That was 100 years after the song was first sung on June 24, 1880.

1981
The personal computer is introduced.

1982
The July 1 national holiday is renamed from Dominion Day to Canada Day.

1983
The UN names 1983 to 1992 as the Decade of Disabled Persons.

14

Law of the Sea

As the country with the longest coastline in the world, Canada has a great deal at stake in ensuring control of the waters around its shorelines. Fishing rights, as well as access to minerals in the deep sea beds or oil and gas reserves under the sea, can cause disputes among countries. As early as 1958, the United Nations held its first Conference on the Law of the Sea. Through the decades, Canada continued to play a leading role in developing an international agreement. The 1982 United Nations Convention on the Law of the Sea (UNCLOS), which Canada ratified in 2003, governs many aspects of use of the sea, including fishing, navigation, marine pollution, and scientific research.

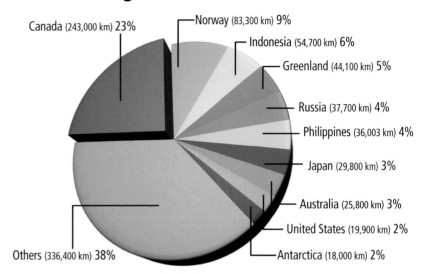

Ten Longest Coastlines in the World

- Canada (243,000 km) 23%
- Norway (83,300 km) 9%
- Indonesia (54,700 km) 6%
- Greenland (44,100 km) 5%
- Russia (37,700 km) 4%
- Philippines (36,003 km) 4%
- Japan (29,800 km) 3%
- Australia (25,800 km) 3%
- United States (19,900 km) 2%
- Antarctica (18,000 km) 2%
- Others (336,400 km) 38%

Coast Guard / Garde côtière

SIR JOHN FRANKLIN

Law of the Sea

1984
Worldwide efforts are aimed at fundraising for Ethiopian famine relief.

1985
A British Antarctic survey team discovers a hole in Earth's ozone layer.

Nansen Award

1986

Nansen Award

In 1986, Canada was awarded the prestigious international humanitarian Nansen Medal for its people's ongoing efforts to help the world's refugees. This was considered a mark of pride for the Canadian people. It was the first time since the medal's inception in 1954 that the United Nations High Commissioner for Refugees awarded it to an entire population. Jeanne Sauvé, governor general at the time, accepted the Nansen Medal on behalf of the People of Canada. It is kept at Rideau Hall in Ottawa, the official home of the Governor General.

1987

Montreal Protocol

In 1987, one of the most important environmental concerns was the depletion of the ozone layer. The ozone layer acts like a type of sunscreen for the planet. It provides an invisible filter that helps to protect all life forms from the Sun's damaging ultraviolet (UV) rays. Canada offered to host a United Nations conference to deal with this problem and other environmental issues. This led to the birth of the Montreal Protocol, an international agreement which prompted countries to take action to stop the depletion of the ozone layer. In describing the effect of the Montreal Protocol, Kofi Annan, former Secretary General of the United Nations, commented that "perhaps the single most successful international agreement to date has been the Montreal Protocol."

TOMS Total Ozone

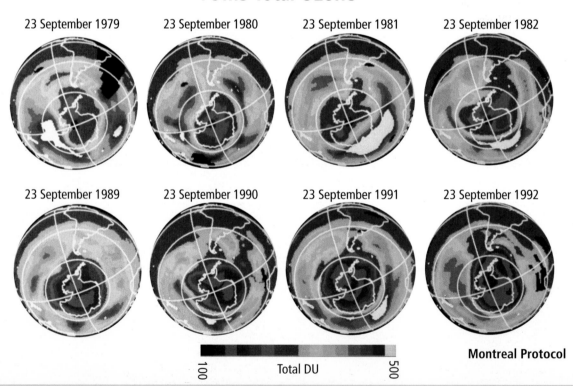

23 September 1979   23 September 1980   23 September 1981   23 September 1982

23 September 1989   23 September 1990   23 September 1991   23 September 1992

100   Total DU   500

Montreal Protocol

1986
The UN General Assembly declares 1986 the "International Year of Peace."

1987
The UN declares International Year of Shelter for the Homeless, a direct result of the Habitat conference in Vancouver in 1976.

Ozone Depletion Process

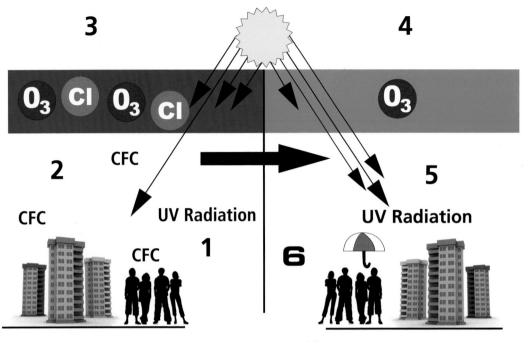

1. CFCs are released into the air.
2. CFCs rise into ozone layer.
3. UV releases Cl from CFCs.
4. Cl destroys ozone.
5. Depleted ozone means more UV.
6. More UV means more skin cancer.

Into the Future

Today, most scientists and governments agree that climate change generated by human activities is one of the largest environmental issues facing the world. Effects of climate change include rising sea levels, stronger seasonal storms, and melting Arctic ice. How would this affect Canada? What can you do to help?

1988
Canada is elected to the UN Security Council.

1989
A free trade agreement between Canada and the United States comes into effect.

1990
The UN Convention on the Rights of the Child becomes enforceable.

1972

UNESCO World Heritage Convention

Some natural or cultural sites are so important to humanity that they should be cared for and protected by the global community. In 1972, the United Nations Educational, Scientific and Cultural Organization (UNESCO), established the World Heritage List. It was part of an international treaty called the Convention Concerning the Protection of the World Cultural and Natural Heritage. By joining the Convention, countries agree to care for the World Heritage Sites in their country. They also agree to avoid any deliberate actions that could damage the sites in other countries. As of 1976, Parks Canada has been responsible for implementing the Convention in Canada.

Since its beginnings in 1972, the World Heritage List has continued to expand. By the mid-2000s, this list included 878 sites worldwide that the World Heritage Committee considered to have outstanding universal value.

1. Canadian Rocky Mountain Parks (Alberta and British Columbia)

2. Dinosaur Provincial Park (Alberta)

3. Gros Morne National Park (Newfoundland and Labrador)

4. Head-Smashed-In Buffalo Jump (Alberta)

5. The Historic District of Old-Quebec (Quebec)

6. Kluane/Wrangell-St Elias/Glacier Bay/Tatshenshini-Alsek (British Columbia, Yukon, and Alaska)

7. L'Anse aux Meadows National Historic Site (Newfoundland and Labrador)

8. Miguasha National Park (Quebec)

9. Nahanni National Park Reserve (Northwest Territories)

10. Old Town Lunenburg (Nova Scotia)

11. Rideau Canal (Ontario)

12. SGang Gwaay (British Columbia)

13. Waterton Glacier International Peace Park (Alberta and Montana)

14. Wood Buffalo National Park (Alberta and Northwest Territories)

UNITED STATES OF AMERICA

YUKON

BRITISH COLUMBIA

ALBERTA

LEGEND

◯ = Natural Landmarks

⬤ = Cultural Sites

SCALE

0 — 269 Kilometres

N W+E S

1971
The International Year for Action to Combat Racism & Racial Discrimination is declared.

1972
Canada co-sponsors the first major international discussion of threats to the environment.

Canada's World Heritage Sites

CANADA

NUNAVUT

NORTHWEST
TERRITORIES

(14)

NEWFOUNDLAND
AND LABRADOR

MANITOBA

(7)

(3)

ASKATCHEWAN

ONTARIO

QUEBEC

PRINCE
EDWARD
ISLAND

(8)

NEW
BRUNSWICK

NOVA
SCOTIA

(5)

(10)

UNITED STATES
OF AMERICA

(11)

1973

The first cellular
phone call is made.

1974

The world population reaches 4 billion people.
By 2009, it had grown to 6.7 billion.

1975

The UN declares International
Women's Year.

19

Habitat Conference

1976

Habitat Conference

In 1976, the first United Nations Habitat Conference was held in Vancouver. At that time, more than one-third of the entire urban population of the developing world lived in slums or squatter settlements. The situation was getting worse each year as more people in the developing world left their farms and rural communities and headed for large cities without having arranged beforehand for a place to live or to work. The first conference, called Habitat 1, was a success in that it brought the issue of adequate shelter to the forefront. The UN continues to hold conferences on human settlement in many cities, including Vancouver again in 2006.

1977

International Women's Day

In 1946, only a year after the UN came into being, one of the first organizations set up was the Commission on the Status of Women. The CSW focusses on the need for equality between men and women. It also works to increase the participation of women around the world in political life, decision-making, the economy, and the environment. In 1975, during its International Women's Year, the United Nations began celebrating March 8 as International Women's Day. Two years later, the UN asked its members to set aside a day each year to promote women's rights and international peace. Following the United Nations' lead, Canada chose March 8 as International Women's Day.

International Women's Day

1976

1977

1979

World Food Day

World Food Day was established by the Food and Agriculture Organization (FAO) of the United Nations in 1979. It is observed in more than 150 countries on October 16, the anniversary of the founding of the FAO in Quebec City in 1945. The FAO was the first specialized agency of the United Nations. This means that it was set up to focus on a specific problem and how to solve it. Through the years, the FAO's goal has always been to help people produce or obtain enough good quality food so they can live healthy, active lives.

World Food Day

Into the Future

Countries, such as Canada, that have signed the World Heritage Convention are able to nominate sites they feel are worthy of inclusion on the World Heritage List. If you were going to nominate a Canadian site, which would you choose? Think about the ways your site has been important to people in the past. What might people in the future learn from your site?

1978
The UN recommends the creation of a division to collect information about UFOs.

1979
The UN International Year of the Child is declared.

1980
The World Health Organization declares smallpox eradicated.

UN Peacekeeping

1961
The International Year of Health and Medical Research is declared.

1962
The United Nations Security Force in West New Guinea is established.

1963
The United Nations Yemen Observation Mission is created.

1960s

UN Peacekeeping

It is often said that Canada invented peacekeeping. This is because, in 1956, Canadian diplomat Lester B. Pearson, who later became Canada's 14th prime minister, devised the idea of a UN multinational peacekeeping force. Peacekeeping activities can take many forms. Sometimes, the primary goal is to keep fighting parties apart by supervising ceasefires. Other peacekeeping missions involve helping people organize or conduct elections. UN peacekeepers have helped to reconstruct roads, clear landmines, and rebuild schools demolished by war. They have helped people to travel safely to see doctors and trained local

police forces. Peacekeeping missions can last a year or less, or, in a very few cases, they can continue for decades. However, just because a country asks the UN to put together a peacekeeping force does not mean that the UN will provide one. The UN Security Council looks at a number of factors before asking member countries to become involved in a peacekeeping force. For example, all the key parties must agree to stop fighting and to accept the UN's role in helping them to resolve their dispute. The UN does not have its own peacekeepers. It asks its member countries to provide the required armed forces and materials. Since 1948, more than 130 nations have contributed military and police personnel to peace operations. Up to one

million soldiers, police officers, and civilians have served under the UN flag since the first peacekeeping operation in 1948. Canada has participated in many of the peacekeeping operations mandated by the United Nations Security Council. By 2009, tens of thousands of Canadians had served in peacekeeping missions in countries around the world. Being a peacekeeper is not an easy job. It requires patience and being able to work among people in conflict without taking sides. Some participants in conflicts do not always want peacekeepers involved. In some cases, peacekeepers have been attacked and have been killed. Other times, peacekeepers get caught in the fighting by mistake.

The First Five UN Peacekeeping Missions

1948 - Following the Israeli War of Independence, the United Nations deployed a peacekeeping team to the Middle East. The purpose of the mission was to supervise a ceasefire between Israel and its Arab neighbours.

1956 - The First United Nations Emergency Force was established to supervise the withdrawal of French, British, and Israeli forces from Egyptian territory.

1949 - The United Nations Military Observer Group in India and Pakistan sends troops to monitor a ceasefire between India and Pakistan.

1958 - The United Nations Observation Group in Lebanon was created to monitor the illegal supply of personnel and arms across Lebanese borders.

1960 - The United Nations Operation in the Congo was established to supervise the withdrawal of Belgian forces from the Congo. In addition, the mission included helping the Congo to maintain political independence, preventing a civil war, maintaining law, and removing all foreign armed forces.

1964
The United Nations Peacekeeping Force in Cyprus is deployed.

1965
UNICEF, the United Nations Children's Fund, is awarded the Nobel Peace Prize.

1965

Adelaide Sinclair Brings Home the Peace Prize

In 1965, UNICEF won the Nobel Peace Prize for its work on behalf of children all over the world. The award ceremony in Norway where the medal is given out was attended by the King and Queen of Norway and high-ranking government leaders and diplomats. UNICEF's Deputy Executive Director for Programmes, a Canadian by the name of Adelaide Sinclair, was also present at the event. After the ceremony, Sinclair was entrusted with bringing the gold Nobel Peace medal back across the Atlantic Ocean for safekeeping.

1967

Outer Space

Many people were amazed in 1957 when they heard about the launch into space of SPUTNIK I, the first artificial satellite. They wondered if people would someday be able to land on the moon, orbit the planets, develop technology for space travel, and if countries would fight to gain control of space. There were many unanswered questions. This led to the 1967 Treaty Governing the Activities of States in the Exploration and Peaceful Uses of Outer Space, Including the Moon and Other Celestial Bodies. Since then, the United Nations has helped coordinate regular conferences and world events to talk about what space development means to humanity. In 1999, the United Nations Office for Outer Space Affairs declared World Space Week, which takes place every year in October.

Outer Space

1966	1967	1968
The UN International Day for the Elimination of Racial Discrimination is declared.	Canada celebrates its 100th year as a nation.	Canada's army, navy, and air force are united as one entity.

Canada and the UN Security Council

Members of the UN Security Council play a very important role in deciding the actions that the UN takes. The Security Council is composed of 15 members. Five members have permanent seats. These are China, France, Russia, the United Kingdom, and the United States. The other 10 seats change every two years. They are held by countries that are elected by other United Nations members according to a formula that takes into consideration where the country is located in the world. Canada first held a seat on the Security Council from 1948 to 1949. Canada has served on the UN Security Council in every decade since then. This includes a term in 1967, which was also Canada's centennial year. Canada's most recent term on the Security Council was from January 1999 to December 2000.

Canada and the UN Security Council

Into the Future

Trying to come to a decision when there are 15 people involved can be very difficult and involve a great deal of discussion. At the UN Security Council, nine members must vote "yes" for a resolution to be adopted. If any one of the five permanent members votes "no," the resolution does not pass. This is known as a "veto," and it dates back to the very beginning of the UN in 1945. Do you think this is a fair system? Can you think of a better way to make decisions?

1969

Canada signs a treaty discouraging the development of nuclear weapons.

1970

Canada joins the World **Intellectual Property** Organization.

UNICEF Canada

1955

UNICEF Canada

Sometimes, schools hold Halloween UNICEF events to help raise money for less fortunate children around the world. Some schools hold pumpkin-carving contests, art auctions with a Halloween theme, or a costume walk. Often called the Trick-or-Treat campaign, these types of events date back to 1955, when a group of volunteers started UNICEF Canada. For many years, children raised money for UNICEF by carrying a little black and orange coin collection box when they went trick and treating. In 2006, this program changed to fundraising activities in schools and through community organizations. Events are held right through the Halloween season. In 2008, the money raised went to the Schools for Africa program for projects in Malawi and Rwanda, continuing the tradition of kids helping kids.

1951

The official home of Canada's prime minister becomes 24 Sussex Drive in Ottawa.

1952

Lester B. Pearson is elected president of seventh session of the UN General Assembly.

Suez Crisis

In 1956, a crisis developed over control of the Suez Canal, a vital shipping link between the Middle East and Europe. The situation grew so heated, with countries taking sides, that world leaders feared it had the potential to develop into another World War. Canadian diplomat Lester B. Pearson devised a solution to resolve the Suez Crisis. He proposed sending an emergency neutral United Nations Peacekeeping force made up of UN member countries under the UN Flag to maintain peace in the region. The United Nations agreed and created the United Nations Emergency Force (UNEF). Around the world, Pearson became a hero for pulling the world back from the brink of war.

Suez Crisis

1953
Elizabeth II becomes queen of Great Britain.

1954
The Nansen Medal humanitarian award is created.

1955
The UN hosts the First International Conference on Peaceful Uses of Nuclear Energy in Geneva.

27

Blue Beret

1956

Blue Beret

The UN peacekeeping Emergency Force was commanded by Canadian E.L.M. Burns. At that time, the uniforms of the Canadian peacekeepers were very similar to those of the British, who were involved in the Suez Crisis conflict. To distinguish the peacekeepers, the decision was made that they would wear a blue beret. Since that time, United Nations peacekeepers have worn blue berets and helmets, so they can be easily identified.

1957

Atomic Energy

Nuclear energy can be used as a weapon. It can also be a valuable technology for scientific development in uses as varied as medicine, electricity, or mining. After World War II, countries worried about nuclear energy's potential for destruction if the world should ever go to war again. In 1957, the International Atomic Energy Agency of the United Nations was set up in Vienna, Austria, with input from a number of countries including Canada. Since its founding the agency has continued its work to promote safe, secure, and peaceful use of nuclear technologies. IAEA operates several regional offices, including one in Toronto.

Atomic Energy

1956

Billy Bishop, a Canadian World War I hero, dies.

1957

Ellen Fairclough, former advisor to Canada's UN delegation, becomes Canada's first female cabinet minister.

1958

The United States creates NASA.

1957

Lester B. "Mike" Pearson

Known for his friendliness and ready smile, Pearson is regarded as the "Grandfather of Modern Peacekeeping." The Nobel Peace Prize Committee recognized his immense contribution to world peace by awarding him the prestigious Peace Prize in 1957. He is the only individual Canadian to ever be awarded this prize.

Lester B. "Mike" Pearson

Into the Future

In 2004, Canadians voted Lester B. Pearson, who went on to become prime minister, as one of the Top 10 Greatest Canadians of all time in a CBC Television nationwide contest. Who would you put on your list of Top 10 Canadians? What was their contribution to Canada? How have these people helped Canada stand out on the international stage?

1959

Canada agrees to shelter hard-to-place refugees during the UN's World Refugee Year.

1960

The Canadian Bill of Rights guarantees civil rights and freedoms to all Canadians.

29

1940s

Allied Nations

UNRRA

1942

Allied Nations

During World War II, representatives of 26 **Allied Nations**, including Canada, met in Washington. At that meeting, U.S. President Roosevelt first used the term "United Nations." He used it in a document called the Declaration by United Nations. The document committed the countries to continuing the fight against the **Axis** Powers together.

1943

UNRRA

By 1943, it was clear that people in many of the European countries affected by the war would need a great deal of assistance after it ended. Looking ahead to the future, a new organization was born. Called the United Nations Relief and Rehabilitation Administration (UNRRA), Canada was directly involved from the outset. Canadian diplomat Lester B. Pearson was elected chairman of the important Supplies Committee, which dealt with the issue of trying to feed millions of people in a time of food shortages. In 1946, he became chairman of the Subcommittee for Displaced Persons, trying to assist people who had lost their homes due to World War II.

1941

The Atlantic Charter, a foundation for many treaties and organizations, declares "all men in all the lands may live out their lives in freedom from want and fear."

1942

The term "United Nations" is first used.

1945

The United Nations Charter

After World War II ended, representatives of 50 countries, including Canadian diplomat Lester B. Pearson, met in San Francisco to draw up the United Nations Charter. This document formed the basis of the United Nations as an international organization. The UN works to keep peace in the world by helping countries to resolve disputes without fighting. The representatives also recognized that many problems and their solutions are universal. For this reason, another of the charter's purposes is to help achieve international cooperation on issues that people face all over the world. These include access to medical care, education, food, and respect for the environment.

The Charter also encourages respect for everyone's human rights and freedoms, regardless of their race, religion, language, or gender.

1943
The need for an international peace and security organization is declared.

1944
The **Commonwealth** Prime Ministers Conference endorses the formation of a peace organization.

1945
UNESCO is founded.

31

1945

United Nations Day

The United Nations officially came into existence on October 24, 1945. By then, the governments of the majority of countries who had signed the charter had also ratified it. Canadians celebrate United Nations Day on 24 October each year.

1948

Universal Declaration of Human Rights

One of the major achievements of the United Nations is the Universal Declaration of Human Rights. It recognizes that the "inherent dignity of all members of the human family is the foundation of freedom, justice and peace in the world." It recognizes that people everywhere are entitled to human rights such as the right to life, freedom and expression, freedom of thought, conscience and religion, and an adequate standard of living. What is so remarkable about the declaration is that it brought together countries with very different politics, religions, and cultures, even some countries that were in conflict. Since 1948, the Universal Declaration has been translated into more than 250 languages. Since the development of the United Nations, Canada has remained committed to the promotion of human rights at home and around the world. This includes being part of the six principal United Nations human rights conventions and covenants.

United Nations Day

1946
UNICEF is set up to help children in countries affected by World War II.

1947
A new oil discovery is made in Leduc, Alberta.

1948
The Universal Declaration of Human Rights is created.

John Peters Humphrey

The principal author of the UN Universal Declaration of Human Rights was a Canadian named John Peters Humphrey. Born in New Brunswick, Humphrey was a scholar, lawyer, and professor at McGill University in Montreal when he was asked to join the UN. He became the first director of the Human Rights Division of the United Nations Secretariat. It was in this role that he wrote the first draft of the document. In 1988, on the 40th anniversary of the declaration, he was awarded the UN's Human Rights award. Humphrey died in 1995 at the age of 89. The John Humphrey Centre for Peace and Human Rights in Edmonton, Alberta honours his memory.

John Peters Humphrey

Into the Future

One of the most important parts of any government is its respect for human rights. Issues such as poverty, equality, and the law can only be fairly addressed when human rights are respected. Today, some of the world's governments do not operate with this respect. Do you think that countries such as Canada, or groups such as the United Nations, have a duty to promote human rights in other countries? If so, how should this be done?

1949

Canada joins the North Atlantic Treaty Organization (NATO).

1950

Canada joins the war in Korea as part of the United Nations force.

1930s

Irene Parlby

1930

Irene Parlby

Since the creation of the League of Nations in 1919, Canada had been represented by a series of talented and dedicated individuals. One of these was Irene Parlby, an elected member and minister in the Alberta Legislature. She also served as a member of the Canadian delegation to the League of Nations in Geneva in 1930. Parlby understood how to stand her ground, and she worked to convince others that what she believed was right and just. She was a member of the Group of Five, a dedicated group of women who fought and succeeded in having women declared as "persons" so they would be eligible to sit in the Canadian Senate.

Statute of Westminster

1931

The League of Nations adopts a General Convention to Improve the Means of Preventing War.

1932

Canada hosts the first Imperial Economic Conference ever held outside London.

1931

Statute of Westminster

Since the end of World War I in 1918, Canada had negotiated and signed international agreements on its own without the assistance of Great Britain. The Statute of Westminster formally put external affairs, also called foreign relations, under the authority of the Canadian government. Foreign relations are Canada's relationships with other countries. In effect, the Statute made it clear that Canada was no longer a colony. Although Canada appeared to the rest of the world as an independent nation with its own symbols, there was one more step to be taken. Even after the British Parliament passed the Statute of Westminster, Canada did not have the power to **amend** its Constitution. That could only be done by the British Parliament. In 1982, Canada, after extensive negotiations with the provinces, requested from Britain the power to amend the Canadian Constitution, and this power was "**repatriated**" to Canada.

1930s

The Great Depression

When the stock markets crashed in Toronto, Montreal, and around the world, Canada plunged into an economic depression that would continue for most of the decade. It was so bad that people called the period the "Dirty Thirties."

The Great Depression

1933
The Great Depression reaches its peak.

1934
The League of Nations discusses a convention for the prevention and punishment of terrorism.

1935
The Bank of Canada opens its doors.

Canada and the Great Depression

Canada's people and economy suffered greatly during the Depression. The Canadian economy depended heavily on exports of its manufactured goods and of natural resources such as logging and mining. When the U.S. economy collapsed, Canadian companies had to start laying off their workers. To make matters worse, during the 1930s, western Canada experienced a severe drought, which caused massive crop failures. In addition, the Depression caused the worldwide price for wheat to fall sharply. Farmers' crops brought farmers so little money that it was hard for them to survive. By 1933, 27 percent of the labour force was unemployed. One in five Canadians had to depend upon government relief. This included work camps for unemployed males. Charities opened soup kitchens where people could come for free soup, a forerunner of food banks. It was not until 1939 when demand for war materials caused a boom in manufacturing that the Great Depression came to an end.

Canada and the Great Depression

1936
The Palais des Nations is constructed in Geneva.

1937
Trans-Canada Airlines is created.

1938
The League of Nations creates the Protection of Civilian Populations Against Bombing From the Air in Case of War.

1939

Canada Goes to War

Throughout the late 1930s, the storm clouds of war had been steadily gathering. On September 3, 1939, Great Britain declared war on Germany. Canada was in a very different position than it was when World War I began in 1914. At that time, since Canada was a member of the British Empire, it had automatically gone to war when Britain did. In contrast, by 1939, Canada had earned the right to make its own decisions on international matters. Prime Minister William Lyon Mackenzie King reassembled Parliament on September 7. The members of Parliament discussed the war and what it would mean for Canada and for the world. Canada declared war on September 10. Canada sent a clear and unmistakable signal to the world that it controlled its own foreign affairs.

Into the Future

In the 1930s, a great many people had difficulty earning money and feeding their families. During hard economic times, it is important that people try to help each other. Are there any groups in your community that exist to help people in distress? Food banks, shelters, and drop-in centres are great ways to help the less fortunate. These groups often can use volunteer help or donations.

1939

The CBC begins special wartime broadcasts.

1940

A Permanent Joint Board of Defence is created by Canada and the United States.

Canada and the United Nations
1920s

1920s

Canada Grows Up

Canada entered the 1920s tired and worn out from World War I. When the war started in August of 1914, people had predicted it would be over by the end of the year. That hope proved to be false. It dragged on until November 1918. Some people say that Canada "came of age" during World War I. Until that time, Canada was largely under Great Britain's control. Great Britain generally spoke on behalf of Canada on international matters. Canada's contribution to World War I brought it international respect and created a new sense of nationalism at home. Throughout the 1920s, Canadian leaders increasingly began to demand, and receive, a Canadian "voice" in world issues.

1921

The Permanent Court of International Justice comes into effect.

1922

Jeanne Sauvé, Canada's first female governor general, is born.

Creating the League of Nations

Creating the League of Nations

World War I has sometimes been called "The War to End All Wars." After World War I, the Peace Conference was held in Paris. World leaders wanted to find a way for countries to resolve their conflicts without resorting to war. Out of these discussions in 1919 came a proposal for the creation of an international organization called the League of Nations. The League was founded on the idea of collective security. It was hoped that international disputes could be resolved by **arbitration**, not through war. With the signing of the Treaty of Versailles, the League of Nations became a reality. The League was headquartered in Geneva, Switzerland. The League's first session was in 1920. Eventually 63 countries, including Canada, joined the League.

Structure of the League of Nations

In a broad sense, the League's structure predicted the future set-up of the United Nations. There was a council, an assembly, and a secretariat. All the members met in the assembly. The council was made up of permanent representatives of the countries that were the major powers of the time, as well as non-permanent representatives elected from among all the other members.

Structure of the League of Nations

1923
Canada's Department of National Defence is created.

1924
The Royal Canadian Air Force is formed.

1925
The League of Nations holds an international health conference.

39

Canada and the League of Nations

Canada was one of the founding members of the League of Nations. In 1927, during Canada's Jubilee Year of Confederation, or Canada's 60th birthday, the members of the League elected Canada to a three-year position on the League's Council. Through the years, Canada took its leadership role at the League very seriously. The Canadian delegation, which represented Canada's viewpoint at meetings, conferences, and in the general assembly, was made up of experienced businesspeople and high-ranking diplomats and politicians. In some years, the prime minister of Canada led the delegation. Canadians also worked in the offices and as administrators for the League. One of them, Herbert Ames, was appointed to the important position of financial director for the League between 1919 and 1926.

`1920s`

Legacy of the League of Nations

The League of Nations held conferences and meetings on a wide range of international concerns from health to economic issues. It also established the Permanent Court of International Justice, where countries could submit international law disputes over such issues as trade, for example. Its successor was the International Court of Justice, established by the United Nations. However, the League failed in its main goal of preserving peace. During the 1930s, the League was not able to deal effectively with armed conflicts or countries trying to take over other countries. World War II began in 1939. While the League had not been successful in preventing war, it did create a format for an international organization such as the United Nations, where countries could work together on global issues. The League of Nations later

1926
The Royal Canadian Legion is formed.

1927
The League of Nation's First International Economic Conference is held at Geneva.

1928
Pier 21 in Halifax greets and evaluates immigrants to Canada.

Legacy of the League of Nations

Halibut Treaty

transferred all its assets to the United Nations. For Canada, the League offered the first large-scale opportunity to talk for itself without Great Britain. The League showed the world that Canada was both willing and able to make its own decisions. At home in Canada, this independent voice helped to create a new nationalism and pride in being Canadian.

1923

Halibut Treaty

Canada has always depended on its natural resources as a backbone of the economy. In the early 1920s, halibut fish stocks were in severe decline in the North Pacific. As a result, Canada and the United States which also fished halibut,

needed to agree on ways to protect the halibut fishery. In 1923, Canada and the United States signed the Halibut Treaty. The treaty was the first treaty Canada ever independently negotiated and signed on its own without Britain. The treaty signalled another step in Canada's independence on the world stage.

Into the Future

If you were going to create a conference to discuss an important issue, what would that issue be? Think about challenges facing the world today. Which of these do you think is the biggest problem? What needs to be dealt with right away, and what can wait? Discuss your choice with friends and family, and discover what they feel is important as well.

1929
The crash of the New York Stock Exchange marks the beginning of the Great Depression.

1930
Canada and the United States raise tariffs on trade goods.

1910s

By the end of the war, 60,661 Canadians had been killed.

1915

In Flanders Fields

In the first few weeks of World War I, thousands of Canadians rushed to join the effort. One of these was Dr. John McRae, a doctor from Guelph, Ontario. By 1915, he was in Ypres, Belgium, in an area known as Flanders. The fighting at Ypres was furious, composed mostly of trench warfare, where soldiers dug deep long trenches into the ground and emerged to fight on open ground. McRae tended the wounded, occasionally manned the guns, and helped with burying the dead. He was inspired to write his famous poem "In Flanders Fields" by the death of his friend, who was buried in a field where wild poppy flowers were just beginning to bloom. McRae died in 1918 at a Canadian military hospital in France. The poem's opening lines "In Flanders fields the poppies blow, Between the crosses, row on row," live on as a symbol of the contributions that Canadians made to World War I.

Safety of Life at Sea

World War I

1913

Safety of Life at Sea

In the 1910s, Canada had very little experience on the world stage. Representatives from Canada had attended only a few conferences where global matters were discussed. One of these was the Conference on the Safety of Life at Sea held in London, England in 1913. Coming just one year after the *Titanic* had hit an iceberg and sunk with great loss of life, the conference's goal was to look for ways to ensure the safety of passengers and crew of oceangoing steamships.

1914

World War I

In 1914, Great Britain declared war on Germany. As a member of the British Empire, Canada was automatically involved. At the time, the total population of Canada was less than 8 million. Still, 628,562 Canadians served in the Canadian armed forces. Of those, 424,589 went overseas.

In Flanders Fields

1913

A total of 400,870 immigrants enter Canada, an all-time high.

1915

Elizabeth Smellie, the first Canadian woman to attain the rank of colonel, begins her military service.

Armistice Day

Each year, the day is marked by parades of Canadian veterans, ceremonies at war memorials, and a moment of silence at 11 a.m.

1919

Paris Peace Conference

The Paris Peace Conference brought a formal end to World War I. Canada had two seats at the Peace Conference, but these were obtained only because Canadian Prime Minister Robert Borden had argued strongly for separate representation for Canada. At first, the British government said it would represent Canada. However, Borden disagreed. He did not want Canada to sit on the sidelines at meetings where important decisions would be made about the future of the world. Borden said that Canada had earned the right to help determine how peace would be established and maintained.

1918

Armistice Day

At the eleventh hour of the eleventh day of the eleventh month of 1918, an armistice was signed that ended World War I fighting. The next year, all across Canada, people at businesses and in schools stopped what they were doing for two minutes at 11 a.m., local time, on November 11, to remember the sacrifices of the soldiers. Even trains and buses came to a complete halt. Until 1931, this time was known as Armistice Day. That year, the name was changed to Remembrance Day, the name by which it is still known today.

Paris Peace Conference

1917
The Military Service Act is passed.

1918
Canadian women over 21 are given the right to vote in federal elections.

1920
The Treaty of Versailles, a peace settlement with Germany, is signed.

43

Canada and the United Nations
1900s

Showing Canada to the World

Canada and the World

1900s

Canada and the World

Canadians greeted the new century with enthusiasm. The economy was booming, and immigration had increased. Canada had been overshadowed by Great Britain and the United States on the world stage. However, many Canadians felt that Canada's time to shine had come. Prime Minister Laurier agreed, saying, "The nineteenth century was the century of the United States. I think we can claim that it is Canada that shall fill the twentieth century."

Canada was a country of which people could be proud. People wondered if its beauty could be shown to their friends and relatives in other parts of Canada and around the world. The answer was a little rectangular cardboard paper known as the "postcard." As of 1897, the Canadian government had allowed private companies to produce picture postcards. Postcards with pictures of major Canadian cities, landscapes, and nature became incredibly popular. In 1900, Canadians sent 27,000 postcards, an impressive number when the country's population was only about five million.

Showing Canada to the World

643I. EMERALD LAKE AND VAN HORN RANGE, B. C.

COPYRIGHT, 1902, BY DETROIT PHOTOGRAPHIC CO.

...ATION IN ILLECILLEWAET GLACIER, B. C.

COPYRIGHT, 1900, BY DETROIT PHOTOGRAPHIC CO.

1900
Edward VII is crowned king of the

1903
A dispute over the Alaskan border leads Canadians

1900s

Canada's Foreign Relations

Even though the United States and Canada shared a border, decisions about their relationship were not decided by Canada. That was because issues between Canada and the United States were considered to be "foreign relations," and these were handled on behalf of Canada by Great Britain. Canadian officials could not talk directly to officials in the United States about fishing or trade or any other cross-border issues. Instead, any negotiations had to involve officials in Great Britain, along with the governor general in Ottawa on behalf of Great Britain, and then, the British Ambassador in Washington. Canada was not allowed to negotiate a boundary with Alaska on its own. Canada had no real say in issues that involved Canadians outside its borders.

Department of External Affairs

Canada's Foreign Relations

1909

Department of External Affairs

In 1904, a new governor general, Earl Grey, was appointed and took office in Ottawa. Many Canadians remember him because he donated the Grey Cup in 1909, which is presented each year to the champion team of what is now known as the Canadian Football League. Canadian diplomats remember him because, under his watch, the Department of External Affairs was set up. Although Canada now had a Department of External Affairs, few people expected that it would actually speak for Canada or make foreign policy decisions about international issues. Instead, its purpose was to create a central location for documents related to foreign affairs. There had previously been no specific policy for dealing with foreign communication, so replies were haphazard or missed altogether. Although it was administrative in nature, the fact that the department was set up was important. It showed Canada's initiative in handling its own relationships with other nations, and that Great Britain was open to the idea of Canadian autonomy.

1907
The National Council of Women of Canada calls for equal pay for work of equal value.

1908
The Royal Canadian Mint is founded in Ottawa.

1910
The Naval Service Act creates a Canadian navy.

45

ACTIVITY
Into the future

The guiding principle of the United Nations is that conflict is best resolved by discussion. Violence, war, and terrorism only exist where diplomacy and ideas have failed. It is the goal of the United Nations to create a world where human rights are respected, where people are treated fairly, and where differences between people and groups are settled peacefully. In order to create such a world, people must learn these ideals, and practise them.

Become a Diplomat

Over the next week, carry a notebook with you. Make notes of the differences of opinion you observe, whether between your friends, on television, or in a newspaper. Think about the different opinions held by the people involved. Make a list of the reasons why each person or party might hold that opinion. As a diplomat, it is your job to find a common ground between these two points of view. With a group of friends, play the roles of the people in disagreement and try to point out what they have in common. You might also imagine a solution to the conflict that would be acceptable to both sides of the debate. This is called a compromise. Compromises are at the core of diplomacy. A well-thought-out compromise can prevent much strife and hardship for the parties involved. Discuss your solutions with friends, family, or classmates to hear their opinions about the issue you have chosen.

FURTHER
Research

Many books and websites provide information on the United Nations. To learn more about this topic, borrow books from the library, or surf the Internet.

Books

Most libraries have computers that connect to a database for researching information. If you input a key word, you will be provided with a list of books in the library that contain information on that topic. Nonfiction books are arranged numerically, using their call number. Fiction books are organized alphabetically by the author's last name.

Websites

To learn more about the United Nations, visit **http://www.un.org/Pubs/CyberSchoolBus/index.shtml**.

For additional information about Canada's role in the UN, read **http://www.unac.org**.

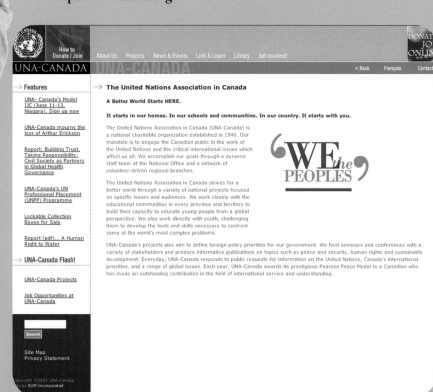

Glossary

Allied Nations: Canada, Great Britain, Australia, the United States, and their military allies during World War II

amend: make changes to a law, treaty, or agreement

arbitration: negotiation between two parties with a neutral third party aiding the process

Axis: the military alliance of Germany, Italy, and Japan during World War II

Commonwealth: a grouping of countries or other bodies

declaration: a formal political statement or announcement

intellectual property: a creative work or invention to which a person owns the rights

moratorium: a ban on the use or production of certain items

ratify: to give official agreement to a treaty or law

reconciliation: repairing a relationship between former adversaries

repatriated: returned to the country of origin

volunteerism: the act of donating one's time and effort to worthy causes

Index

J 341.237 CLI
33292011934431
wpa
Cline, Beverly Fink, 1951-
Canada and the United